P9-CQR-070

Pebble® Plus

EXtreme Animals

The Best

Camouflaged Animals

by Megan Cooley Peterson

Consulting Editor: Gail Saunders-Smith, PhD

Consultant: Tanya Dewey, PhD
University of Michigan Museum of Zoology

CAPSTONE PRESS
a capstone imprint

Pebble Plus is published by Capstone Press,
1710 Roe Crest Drive, North Mankato, Minnesota 56003.
www.capstonepub.com

Books published by Capstone Press are manufactured with paper
containing at least 10 percent post-consumer waste.

Library of Congress Cataloging-in-Publication Data
Peterson, Megan Cooley.
  The best camouflaged animals / by Megan Cooley Peterson.
    p. cm.—(Pebble Plus. Extreme animals)
  Includes bibliographical references and index.
  Summary: "Simple text and photographs present some of the world's best-camouflaged animals"—Provided
by publisher.
  ISBN 978-1-4296-7599-4 (library binding)
  ISBN 978-1-4296-7902-2 (paperback)
  1. Camouflage (Biology)—Juvenile literature. I. Title. II. Series.
QL759.P49 2012
591.47'2—dc23   2011026935

Editorial Credits
Katy Kudela, editor; Heidi Thompson, set designer; Alison Thiele, book designer; Svetlana Zhurkin, media researcher;
    Kathy McColley, production specialist

Photo Credits
Dreamstime: Image Focus, 19, Mark Lotterhand, 9, Shmer (camouflage texture), 4, 10, 16; iStockphoto: David Parsons,
7; Minden Pictures: npl/Brent Hedges, cover, 12–13; National Geographic Stock: Paul Nicklen, 5; Photolibrary:
Nick Garbutt, 20–21; Photo Researchers: John Shaw, 11; Shutterstock: Doug James, 1, Stephan Kerkhofs, 16–17,
Stubblefield Photography, 14–15

Note to Parents and Teachers

The Extreme Animals series supports national science standards related to life science.
This book describes and illustrates camouflaged animals. The images support early readers
in understanding the text. The repetition of words and phrases helps early readers learn new
words. This book also introduces early readers to subject-specific vocabulary words, which are
defined in the Glossary section. Early readers may need assistance to read some words and to
use the Table of Contents, Glossary, Read More, Internet Sites, and Index sections of the book.

Printed in the United States of America in North Mankato, Minnesota.
102011   006405CGS12

Table of Contents

Good Camouflage

They hide! They change colors!

They are plain hard to see!

These hide-and-seek masters take

camouflage to the EXTREME.

In winter, Arctic foxes' thick,

white fur blends in with the snow.

These hunters sneak up on prey.

In summer, their fur turns brown.

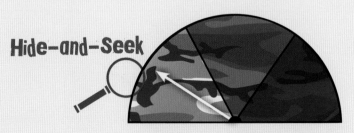

Hide-and-Seek

Camo Meter

Horned lizards' colors blend in with the deserts they call home. Ants, beetles, and spiders don't see them until it's too late.

Goldenrod crab spiders hide on white and yellow flowers. They change colors to match the petals. Chomp! They catch insects by surprise.

Great Camouflage

A dead leaf butterfly darts away
from a hungry bird. The butterfly
lands and closes its wings.
The bird thinks the butterfly
is a dead leaf.

Out of
Sight

Hide-and-Seek

Camo Meter

Leafy sea dragons swim slowly through the seaweed to stay safe. Long pieces of skin grow from their bodies. The pieces look like seaweed.

sea dragon

13

A mimic octopus hides in plain sight! It can change its color and shape. Eeek! Now it looks like deadly sea snakes. Predators are too afraid to eat this octopus.

Amazing Camouflage

A stonefish hides in a coral reef.

Its bumpy body looks like stone.

It waits for small fish to swim by.

Then it gobbles up the fish.

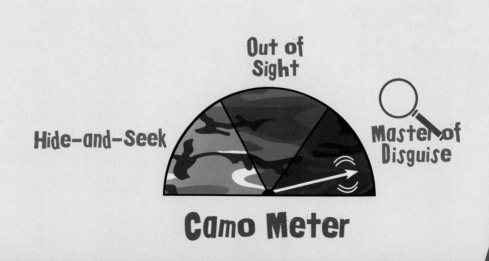

Out of
Sight

Hide-and-Seek

Master of
Disguise

Camo Meter

stonefish

A hungry dolphin swims near
a cuttlefish. In a blink,
the cuttlefish changes color.
It blends in with the coral reef
to stay safe.

cuttlefish

Freeze! A great potoo holds still.

Its gray and white feathers

look like tree bark.

Predators think this bird

is a tree branch.